P9-DTP-144

United States Presidents

CONTRA COSTA COUNTY LIBRARY

Rutherford B. Hayes

Anne Welsbacher

ABDO Publishing Company

3 1901 03534 9093

visit us at
www.abdopub.com

Published by ABDO Publishing Company, 4940 Viking Drive, Edina, Minnesota 55435.
Copyright © 2001 by Abdo Consulting Group, Inc. International copyrights reserved in all countries. No part of this book may be reproduced in any form without written permission from the publisher.

Published 2001
Printed in the United States of America.
Second printing 2002

Photo credits: Corbis

Contributing editors: Tamara L. Britton and Christine Phillips
Book design and graphics: Patrick Laurel

Library of Congress Cataloging-in-Publication Data

Welsbacher, Anne, 1955-
   Rutherford B. Hayes / Anne Welsbacher.
     p. cm. -- (United States presidents)
   Includes index.
   Summary: Describes the life and career of the Civil War general and Ohio politician who became the nineteenth president of the United States.
    ISBN 1-57765-248-7
    1. Hayes, Rutherford Birchard, 1822-1893--Juvenile literature. 2. Presidents--United States--Biography--Juvenile literature. [1. Hayes, Rutherford Birchard, 1822-1893. 2. Presidents.] I. Title. II. Series: United States presidents (Edina, Minn.)
E682.W45 2000
973.8'3'092--dc21
   [B]   98-30123
                                       CIP
                                        AC

Contents

Rutherford B. Hayes 4

Early Years 8

Serious Student 10

Law and Marriage 12

Civil War Soldier 14

The Making of the Nineteenth
     United States President 16

Representative Hayes.. 18

Governor Hayes 20

President Hayes 22

The Seven "Hats" of the U.S. President 26

The Three Branches of the U.S. Government... 27

Later Years 28

Glossary 30

Internet Sites 31

Index 32

Rutherford B. Hayes

*R*utherford B. Hayes became the nineteenth president in 1877. He won the most contested election in U.S. history.

Hayes was born in Ohio. His father died before he was born. His brother died when he was two years old. His best friend was his sister Fanny.

Hayes was a serious student. After he graduated from college, he became a **lawyer**. Hayes married Lucy Ware Webb. They had eight children.

During the **Civil War**, Hayes joined the army. He fought bravely in many battles. He was **promoted** to **major general**.

After the war, he became a member of the U.S. **House of Representatives**. Later, he became governor of Ohio.

During his presidency, Hayes ended **Reconstruction**. He worked to end the **spoils system**. And he worked for civil service **reform**. He died of a heart attack in 1893.

President Rutherford B. Hayes

Rutherford B. Hayes (1822-1893)
Nineteenth President

BORN:	October 4, 1822
PLACE OF BIRTH:	Delaware, Ohio
ANCESTRY:	English-Scot
FATHER:	Rutherford Hayes (1787-1822)
MOTHER:	Sophia Birchard Hayes (1792-1866)
WIFE:	Lucy Ware Webb (1831-1889)
CHILDREN:	Eight: seven boys, one girl
EDUCATION:	Norwalk Academy, Isaac Webb's prep school, Kenyon College, Harvard Law School
RELIGION:	Methodist
OCCUPATION:	Lawyer, soldier
MILITARY SERVICE:	Ohio Twenty-third Volunteers
POLITICAL PARTY:	Democrat

OFFICES HELD:	City attorney of Cincinnati, U.S. House of Representatives, governor of Ohio
AGE AT INAUGURATION:	54
YEARS SERVED:	1877-1881
VICE PRESIDENT:	William A. Wheeler
DIED:	January 17, 1893, Fremont, Ohio, age 70
CAUSE OF DEATH:	Heart attack

**Birthplace of
Rutherford B. Hayes**

Early Years

*R*utherford Birchard Hayes was born on October 4, 1822, in Delaware, Ohio. His **nickname** was Rud. He was the fourth child of Sophia Birchard and Rutherford Hayes Jr. Rud's father owned a farm.

Rud had an older brother and sister, Lorenzo and Fanny. His older sister Sarah died when she was very young. Rud's father died three months before he was born.

Rud's uncle, Sardis Birchard, helped Sophia raise Rud, Lorenzo, and Fanny. Later, Birchard built a big house for the family called Spiegel Grove.

When Rud was two, Lorenzo drowned. So Sophia became very protective of Rud and Fanny.

Fanny and Rud stayed home with Sophia. They did not go to school. So they became very close. Fanny was Rud's best friend.

Rud and Fanny ran in the fields, went swimming and fishing, and played baseball. Neighbors did not think Fanny should play like a boy. But Rud and Fanny were happy.

Spiegel Grove in Fremont, Ohio

Serious Student

*I*n 1836, Rud went to Norwalk Academy in Norwalk, Ohio. He studied speaking and writing. During the summer, Rud was **tutored** in Greek and Latin. Fanny taught him to speak French.

The next year, Rud went to Isaac Webb's prep school in Middletown, Connecticut. He was a good student. He enjoyed living in New England. Webb thought Rud should spend another year in prep school. But Rud wanted to return to Ohio.

Rud's mother wanted him to come home, too. So in 1838, Rud went to Kenyon College in Gambier, Ohio.

In 1842, Rud graduated from college. He was class **valedictorian**. He decided he wanted to be a **lawyer**.

Rud went to Harvard Law School. He graduated in 1845. That same year, he passed the **bar exam**. Now he could begin work as a lawyer.

Kenyon College in Gambier, Ohio

Law and Marriage

*H*ayes opened his law firm in Lower Sandusky, Ohio. His cases were usually **debt** collection and land sales.

In April 1846, he became partners with Ralph Buckland. Hayes got more experience working with Buckland. And he liked working with a partner.

In May 1846, the **Mexican War** began. Hayes wanted to join the army. But he had a sore throat. So his doctor said he was not well enough. Hayes went to Fanny's house in Cincinnati to get better.

Hayes visited Ohio Wesleyan University in 1847. There he met Lucy Ware Webb. They became friends. They wrote each other letters. And they occasionally went out together.

In 1849, Hayes moved to Cincinnati. At first, he did not make much money. But soon his law firm was successful.

Lucy Webb graduated from college in 1851. She and Hayes were married on December 30, 1852.

In 1853, they had their first child. In all, they had eight children. But three died while they were young.

In 1856, Hayes founded Ohio's first **Republican** party branch. His law firm was doing well. He defended runaway slaves. He also had three famous murder cases. That same year, his sister Fanny died.

In 1858, Hayes became Cincinnati's city **attorney**. He represented the city in lawsuits and advised city offices on the law. He was re-elected in 1859.

Lucy Webb Hayes

Civil War Soldier

*D*uring this time, the North and South were fighting over slavery. The North wanted to end slavery. The South thought each state should have slavery if it wanted to.

In 1860, Abraham Lincoln was elected president. He did not like slavery. So many Southern states **seceded**. They formed a country called the **Confederate States of America**. The Northern states were called the **Union**.

In April 1861, the Confederacy attacked Fort Sumter in South Carolina. This event started the **Civil War**.

On June 7, 1861, Hayes joined the Union army. He was a major with the Twenty-third Ohio Volunteers. He fought in West Virginia and Virginia.

Hayes liked being in the army. He was proud to fight for freedom for all people. He was **promoted** to **lieutenant colonel** and then to colonel.

In September 1862, he was wounded at the Battle of South Mountain. So he could not fight in the Battle of Antietam. He was disappointed.

Hayes went to an army hospital in Maryland. Lucy's brother, Dr. Joseph Webb, treated his injury. Lucy came to visit him. Soon he returned to the war.

In October 1864, he was elected to the U.S. **House of Representatives**. But Hayes stayed in the army until the war was over.

On April 9, 1865, the **Confederacy surrendered**. On April 14, John Wilkes Booth shot President Lincoln to **avenge** the South. Lincoln died the next day. Vice President Andrew Johnson became president.

On June 7, 1865, Hayes was **discharged** from the army. Then he was **promoted** to **major general**.

A picture of Lieutenant Colonel Hayes taken during the Civil War

The Making of the Nineteenth United States President

1822
Born October 4

1842
Graduates from Kenyon College

1845
Graduates from Harvard Law School

1846
Mexican War begins

1847
Meets Lucy Webb

1858
Elected city attorney

1859
Re-elected city attorney

1860
Abraham Lincoln elected president

1861
Civil War begins; joins Union army

1862
Wounded at Battle of South Mountain

1867
Resigns from House of Representatives; elected Ohio governor

1869
Re-elected governor

1870
Fifteenth Amendment added to Constitution

1875
Re-elected governor

Rutherford B. Hayes

". . . he serves his party best who serves his country best."

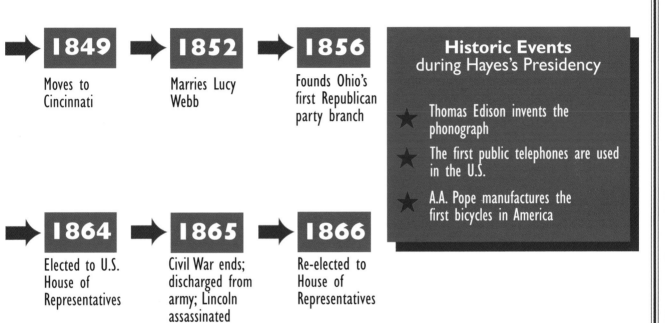

1849

Moves to Cincinnati

1852

Marries Lucy Webb

1856

Founds Ohio's first Republican party branch

Historic Events
during Hayes's Presidency

★ Thomas Edison invents the phonograph

★ The first public telephones are used in the U.S.

★ A.A. Pope manufactures the first bicycles in America

1864

Elected to U.S. House of Representatives

1865

Civil War ends; discharged from army; Lincoln assassinated

1866

Re-elected to House of Representatives

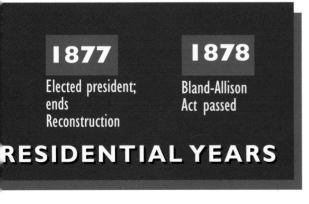

1877

Elected president; ends Reconstruction

1878

Bland-Allison Act passed

1889

Wife Lucy dies

1893

Dies January 17

RESIDENTIAL YEARS

Representative Hayes

*I*n December 1865, Hayes joined the U.S. **House of Representatives**. At this time, President Johnson had to bring the **Confederate** states back into the **Union**. This is called **Reconstruction**.

Johnson favored an easy reunion. In his plan, each state had to write a new **constitution**. It had to repeal its act of **secession**. And it had to approve the Thirteenth **Amendment**, which outlawed slavery.

President Andrew Johnson

In **Congress**, Radical **Republicans** wanted a tougher plan. They wanted to protect the freed slaves' civil rights. Hayes was a Radical Republican.

Hayes voted for the Freedmen's Bureau Act. It gave food, medicine, and education to freed slaves in the South. He also voted for the Fourteenth Amendment. It made all freed slaves U.S. citizens.

In 1866, Hayes was re-elected. In 1867, he voted for the **Reconstruction** Acts.

In these acts, the Southern states had to elect new governments. They had to draft new **constitutions** that promised voting rights for all men. And they had to approve the Fourteenth **Amendment**.

Secretary of War Edwin Stanton made sure the army enforced the

Edwin Stanton

Reconstruction Acts. **Congress** was afraid that President Johnson would fire Stanton and enforce his own Reconstruction plan.

So Hayes voted for the Tenure of Office Act. It made it illegal for the president to fire **cabinet** members without **Senate** approval.

President Johnson fired Stanton anyway. Many congressmen thought Johnson should be **impeached**. Hayes agreed.

But the congressional session ended. Hayes went back to Ohio to campaign for governor. When President Johnson was impeached in 1868, Hayes was not there to vote. He **resigned** from the **House of Representatives** on August 7, 1867.

Governor Hayes

*O*n October 8, 1867, the people of Ohio elected Hayes governor. As governor, Hayes worked to change the **spoils system**. He hired the best people for the job, whether they were **Republicans** or not.

Hayes worked for prison **reform**. And he oversaw the construction of a school for deaf children.

In Ohio, Hayes passed the Fifteenth **Amendment**. It gave freed slaves the right to vote.

Hayes worked to end laws that denied the right to vote to mixed-race people. But he did not support women's right to vote.

In 1869, Hayes was re-elected. He worked on Ulysses S. Grant's presidential campaign. He also supported building a state university.

That same year, Hayes ordered a **geologic** survey of Ohio. He wanted to study Ohio's mineral **resources**. Hayes knew Ohio needed more mining and manufacturing to remain successful.

In 1870, the Fifteenth **Amendment** was added to the U.S. **Constitution**. And construction began on Ohio Agricultural and Mechanical College. It became Ohio State University.

In 1875, Hayes was elected for a third term. But on June 14, 1876, the **Republican** party **nominated** him for president. The **Democrats** chose Samuel Tilden.

President Ulysses S. Grant

President Hayes

*T*he election was held on November 7, 1876. Tilden had 184 **electoral votes** and Hayes had 165. To win, a candidate needed 185 electoral votes.

But the election results in Louisiana, South Carolina, and Florida were contested. Some people voted more than once. Some people who could not read were tricked into voting for the wrong candidate.

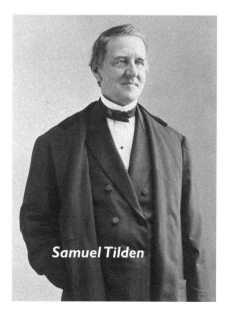

Samuel Tilden

In December, **Congress** established an Electoral Commission. It had eight **Republicans** and seven **Democrats**. They voted to decide which candidate got the contested votes. After much discussion, they gave all the votes to Hayes.

On March 2, 1877, the electoral votes were counted. Hayes had 185 and Tilden had 184. Hayes won the election.

Louisiana and South Carolina still had **Republican** governments established by the **Reconstruction** Acts. The U.S. Army supported these governments.

Hayes withdrew the army from these states. This ended **Civil War** Reconstruction.

Hayes also kept working to end the **spoils system**. Many Republicans were upset when Hayes named David Key postmaster general. Key was a **Democrat**. He was also a colonel in the **Confederate** army.

Chester A. Arthur became the twenty-first U.S. president.

Then Hayes fired Republicans Chester A. Arthur and Alonzo B. Cornell from the New York Customhouse. Hayes felt that they gave jobs to unqualified people.

Hayes wanted to **reform** civil service, too. In June 1877, he forbade civil servants from participating in politics.

Hayes supported the gold standard. He wanted to trade the paper dollars issued during the **Civil War** for gold dollars.

Some people thought dollars should be made from silver, too. So in 1878, **Congress** proposed the Bland-Allison Act. This act allowed the U.S. to make four million silver dollars a month.

President James A. Garfield

Hayes felt that silver was worth less than gold. So he felt it was not fair to repay money that was borrowed in gold dollars with silver dollars.

Hayes **vetoed** the act. But Congress overrode his veto and the act became law.

One term was enough for Hayes. In 1880, James A. Garfield was elected president. Hayes moved back home to Ohio.

The United States during Hayes's presidency

Existing States

Existing Territories

The Seven "Hats" of the U.S. President

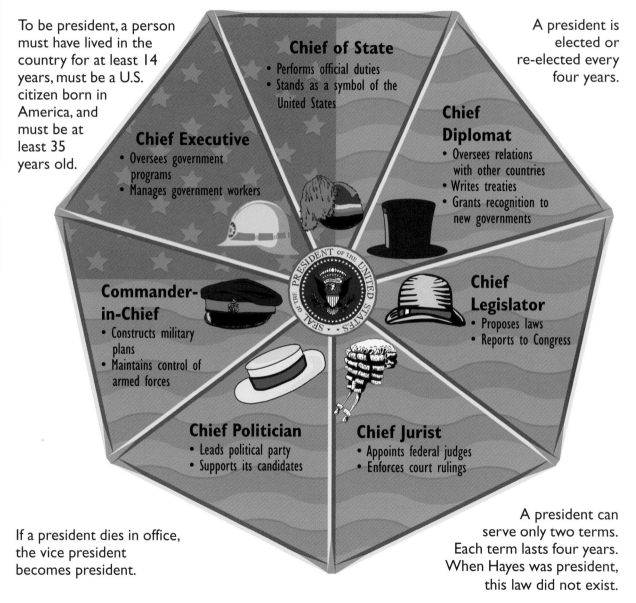

To be president, a person must have lived in the country for at least 14 years, must be a U.S. citizen born in America, and must be at least 35 years old.

A president is elected or re-elected every four years.

Chief of State
- Performs official duties
- Stands as a symbol of the United States

Chief Diplomat
- Oversees relations with other countries
- Writes treaties
- Grants recognition to new governments

Chief Executive
- Oversees government programs
- Manages government workers

Commander-in-Chief
- Constructs military plans
- Maintains control of armed forces

Chief Legislator
- Proposes laws
- Reports to Congress

Chief Politician
- Leads political party
- Supports its candidates

Chief Jurist
- Appoints federal judges
- Enforces court rulings

If a president dies in office, the vice president becomes president.

A president can serve only two terms. Each term lasts four years. When Hayes was president, this law did not exist.

As president, Rutherford B. Hayes had seven jobs.

The Three Branches
of the U.S. Government

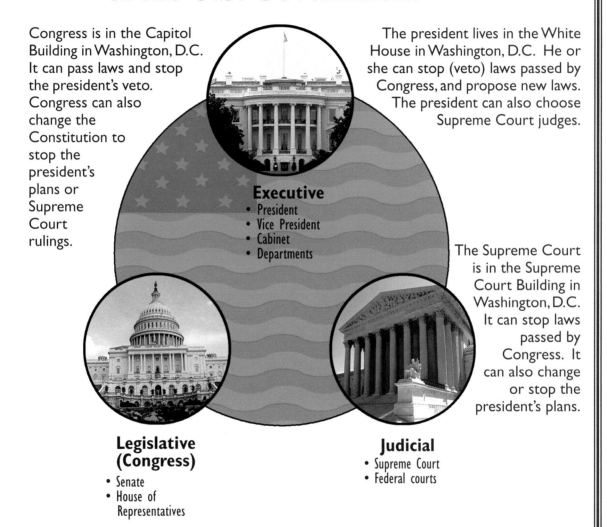

Congress is in the Capitol Building in Washington, D.C. It can pass laws and stop the president's veto. Congress can also change the Constitution to stop the president's plans or Supreme Court rulings.

The president lives in the White House in Washington, D.C. He or she can stop (veto) laws passed by Congress, and propose new laws. The president can also choose Supreme Court judges.

Executive
- President
- Vice President
- Cabinet
- Departments

The Supreme Court is in the Supreme Court Building in Washington, D.C. It can stop laws passed by Congress. It can also change or stop the president's plans.

Legislative (Congress)
- Senate
- House of Representatives

Judicial
- Supreme Court
- Federal courts

The U.S. Constitution formed three government branches. Each branch has power over the others. So no single group or person can control the country. The Constitution calls this "separation of powers."

Later Years

*B*ack in Ohio, Hayes worked to support Western Reserve, Ohio Wesleyan, and Ohio State Universities. He worked with the Slater Fund to raise money for the education of poor children and African-Americans.

Hayes also felt that **reforming** criminals was part of education. So he continued working to improve the prison system.

Hayes also served as a bank president. Once a year, he met with other **Civil War veterans**. And he joined the New York Civil Service Reform Association.

In 1889, he and Lucy took a trip to New York City. Later that year, Lucy died of a stroke. Hayes missed her. He stayed busy and enjoyed his family's company. In 1890, he went to Burmuda with his daughter Fanny.

On January 14, 1893, Hayes had a heart attack. He was traveling, but he took a train to Spiegel Grove. He wanted to die at home. He died there on January 17, 1893.

Rutherford B. Hayes fought bravely in the **Civil War**. He worked to secure rights for African Americans. He supported public education, civil service **reform**, and ending the **spoils system**. Hayes was an important American leader.

Hayes Hall at Ohio State University. Hayes was a founder of the school, and became its board president in 1892.

Glossary

Amendment - a change to the Constitution of the United States.

attorney - another name for lawyer.

avenge - to get revenge for.

bar exam - the test a person must pass to become a lawyer.

cabinet - a group of advisers chosen by the president.

Civil War - a war between groups in the same country. The United States of America and the Confederate States of America fought a civil war from 1861 to 1865.

Confederate States of America - the country formed by the 11 states that left the Union between 1860 and 1861. It is also called the Confederacy.

Congress - the lawmaking body of the U.S. It is made up of the Senate and the House of Representatives.

Constitution - the document that states the supreme law in the United States. Each state has a constitution, too.

debt - something owed to someone, usually money.

Democrat - a political party. During Hayes's presidency, Democrats were conservative and supported farming and landowners.

discharge - to be released from military service.

electoral votes - votes cast by the electoral college. The electoral college is a group that elects the president and vice president. After a presidential election, each state sends its representatives to the electoral college. There, they vote for their party's candidate.

geology - the study of rocks and minerals in the earth. A geologic survey is a report on the rocks and minerals found in an area.

House of Representatives - a group of people elected by citizens to represent them. It meets in Washington, D.C., to make laws for the nation. Most states have a House of Representatives to make state laws.

impeach - to have a trial to decide if a civil servant should be removed from office.

lawyer - someone who knows the laws and acts for another person in a court of law.

lieutenant colonel - an army rank above major and below colonel.

major general - an army rank above brigadier general and below lieutenant general.

Mexican War - a war between the U.S. and Mexico between 1846 and 1848.

nickname - a name that in some way describes a person, that is used instead of his or her real name.

nominate - to name a candidate for office.

promote - to move up in rank or position.

Reconstruction - the period of time after the Civil War when laws were passed to help the Southern states rebuild and return to the Union.

reform - to change something to make it better.

Republican - a political party. When Hayes was president, they supported business and strong government.

resign - to quit.

resources - a natural source of wealth.

secede - to leave a group.

secretary of war - the adviser to the president who handles the nation's defense.

Senate - a group of 100 elected senators, two from each state, that make laws for the country.

spoils system - a system of giving people jobs or taking them away because of political beliefs.

surrender - to give up.

tutor - to be taught by a private teacher. The teacher is also called a tutor.

Union - the states that remained part of the U.S. during the Civil War.

valedictorian - the highest-ranking student in a class. The valedictorian gives a speech at graduation.

veteran - a person who served in the armed forces.

veto - to keep a law from passing. Veto is a special power held by the president. Congress can override a veto with a two-thirds majority vote.

Internet Sites

The Presidents of the United States of America
http://www.whitehouse.gov/WH/glimpse/presidents.html
This site is from the White House.

PBS American Presidents Series
http://www.americanpresidents.org
This site from PBS has links and information about Hayes's life.

Rutherford B. Hayes Presidential Center
http://www.rbhayes.org
This site includes links to Hayes's home, his presidential library, museum, and more.

These sites are subject to change. Go to your favorite search engine and type in United States Presidents for more sites.

Index

A

Arthur, Chester A. 23

B

Birchard, Sardis 8
birth 4, 8
Bland-Allison Act 24
Booth, John Wilkes 15
Buckland, Ralph 12

C

children 4, 12, 28
city attorney 13
Civil War 4, 14, 15, 23, 24, 28, 29
Confederate States of America 14, 15, 18, 23
Congress 18, 19, 22, 24
Cornell, Alonzo B. 23

D

death 4, 28

E

education 4, 8, 10
Electoral Commission 22

F

Fifteenth Amendment 20, 21
Fourteenth Amendment 18, 19
Freedmen's Bureau Act 18

G

Garfield, James A. 24
governor 4, 19, 20, 21
Grant, Ulysses S. 20

H

Hayes, Lucy Webb (wife) 4, 12, 15, 28
health 12, 15, 28
hobbies 8
House of Representatives, U.S. 4, 15, 18, 19

J

Johnson, Andrew 15, 18, 19

K

Key, David 23

L

lawyer 4, 10, 12, 13
Lincoln, Abraham 14, 15

M

Mexican War 12
military service 4, 14, 15

O

Ohio State University 21, 28
Ohio Wesleyan University 12, 28

P

parents 4, 8, 10
president 4, 21, 22, 23, 24
presidential election 4, 22

R

Radical Republicans 18
Reconstruction 4, 18, 19, 23
Reconstruction Acts 19, 23

S

Senate 19
siblings 4, 8, 12, 13
Slater Fund 28
slavery 13, 14, 18, 20
spoils system 4, 20, 23, 29
Stanton, Edwin 19

T

Tenure of Office Act 19
Thirteenth Amendment 18
Tilden, Samuel 21, 22

U

Union 14, 18

W

Webb, Isaac 10
Webb, Joseph 15
Western Reserve 28